WATER AND ROCK

HOW
THE GRAND CANYON
FORMED

THERESA EMMINIZER

PowerKiDS
press.
New York

Published in 2020 by The Rosen Publishing Group, Inc.
29 East 21st Street, New York, NY 10010

First Edition

Editor: Sarah Machajewski
Book Design: Tanya Dellaccio

Photo Credits: Cover Dean Fikar/Moment/Getty Images; p. 4 https://upload.wikimedia.org/wikipedia/commons/1/1c/President_Roosevelt_-_Pach_Bros.jpg; p. 5 Anton_Ivanov/Shutterstock.com; p. 6 William Eugene Dummitt/Shutterstock.com; p. 7 Galyna Andrushko/Shutterstock.com; p. 9 https://upload.wikimedia.org/wikipedia/commons/d/d6/Grand_Canyon_National_Park-_The_Kaibab_from_South_Kaibab_Trail.jpg; p. 11 Adwo/Shutterstock.com; p. 13 (top) Jin Foltyn/Shutterstock.com; p. 13 (bottom) BSIP/Universal Images Group/Getty Images; p. 15 (top) Demetrio Carrasco/Getty Images; p. 15 (bottom) D Gentilcore/Shutterstock.com; p. 17 George Rose/Getty Images News/Getty Images; p. 19 Beth Ruggiero-York/Shutterstock.com; p. 20 Fernando Tatay/Shutterstock.com; p. 21 mariakraynova/Shutterstock.com; p. 23 (both) Francisco Blanco/Shutterstock.com; p. 25 Bettmann/Getty Images; p. 27 (top) Matt Crisman/Shutterstock.com; p. 27 (bottom) Tom Grundy/Shutterstock.com; p. 29 Joe Sohm/Visions of America/Universal Images Group/Getty Images; p. 30 Harold Stiver/EyeEm/Getty Images.

Library of Congress Cataloging-in-Publication Data

Names: Emminizer, Theresa, author.
Title: Water and rock : how the Grand Canyon formed / Theresa Emminizer.
Description: New York : PowerKids Press, [2020] | Series: Earth's history
  through rocks | Includes index.
Identifiers: LCCN 2018060240| ISBN 9781725301641 (pbk.) | ISBN 9781725301665
  (library bound) | ISBN 9781725301658 (6 pack)
Subjects: LCSH: Basins (Geology)-Juvenile literature. | Landforms-Juvenile
  literature. | Geology-Arizona-Grand Canyon-Juvenile literature. | Grand
  Canyon (Ariz.)-Juvenile literature.
Classification: LCC QE615 .E46 2020 | DDC 557.91/32-dc23
LC record available at https://lccn.loc.gov/2018060240

Manufactured in the United States of America

CPSIA Compliance Information: Batch #CSPK19. For Further Information contact Rosen Publishing, New York, New York at 1-800-237-9932.

CONTENTS

A NATIONAL TREASURE

The Grand Canyon is an **iconic** American landmark. Its historic, **cultural**, and geological importance make it one of the most **unique** places in the world. Home to 12,000-year-old human **artifacts** from the Paleo-Indian period, 2-billion-year-old rocks, and countless fossils, this natural wonder has so much importance that it has been given special protection under the law as a World **Heritage** Site.

The massive size of the Grand Canyon makes it a sight to behold. Every year, hundreds of thousands of tourists are drawn to its wonders. The Grand Canyon measures 277 miles (445.8 km) long, 18 miles (29 km) wide in some areas, and a mile (1.6 km) deep. How exactly was this mighty canyon created? The story lies within the rocks.

A "GREAT WONDER OF NATURE"

President Theodore Roosevelt first visited the Grand Canyon in 1903. During his presidency, he was committed to creating laws that would protect the landmark. In 1908, he said: "Let this great wonder of nature remain as it now is. You cannot improve on it. But what you can do is keep it for your children, your children's children, and all who come after you, as the one great sight which every American should see."

READING THE ROCKS

ALTHOUGH IT DOESN'T INCLUDE THE WHOLE CANYON, GRAND CANYON NATIONAL PARK IS 1,904 SQUARE MILES (4,931.3 SQ. KM). THAT'S BIGGER THAN RHODE ISLAND!

The public has access to two areas of Grand Canyon National Park. The South Rim is about 7,000 feet (2,133.6 m) above sea level and the North Rim is 8,000 feet (2,438.4 m) above sea level.

5

THE BASEMENT ROCKS

The oldest rocks in the Grand Canyon are nearly 2 billion years old. They're called the Vishnu Basement Rocks. These rocks make up the lowest rock layer in the canyon. The Vishnu Basement Rocks are metamorphic and igneous rocks. They include schist, gneiss, and granite.

Between 1.68 billion and 1.84 billion years ago, part of the continent that's now North America crashed into volcanic islands. The basement rocks formed in this crash. The heat and pressure from the crash created rock called Vishnu schist.

The schist had tiny cracks throughout it. Molten rock from deep inside Earth flowed up through the layers of the planet and seeped through the cracks in the schist. The molten rock cooled and hardened. This created a pink rock called Zoroaster granite.

You can see the pink Zoroaster granite and gray Vishnu schist in this canyon rock in the inner gorge.

IGNEOUS, SEDIMENTARY, AND METAMORPHIC

There are three kinds of rocks: igneous, sedimentary, and metamorphic. Rocks are sorted into these groups based on how they formed. Igneous rocks form when molten rock cools and hardens. Sedimentary rocks form when sediments—or small pieces of sand, soil, or mud—pile into layers and are pressed together over time. Metamorphic rocks are igneous and sedimentary rocks that have been changed by heat and pressure.

7

LAYERS OF SEDIMENT

Layers of sedimentary rock sit on top of the basement rock. These layers formed over millions of years. One of the things that's special about the Grand Canyon is that each of these distinct rock layers is visible in the canyon's walls!

People have identified, dated, and named the Grand Canyon's sedimentary rock layers. The lowest layer, which sits on top of the basement rock, is composed of the Grand Canyon Supergroup Rocks. Above them are the Tapeats Sandstone layer and the Bright Angel Shale, which formed about 515 million years ago. On top of the shale are the Muav Limestone, Temple Butte Formation, Redwall Limestone, the Supai Group, Hermit Shale, Coconino Sandstone, and Toroweap Formation. The youngest layer of rocks is right at the top. It is called the Kaibab Limestone.

The youngest rocks in the Grand Canyon are 270 million years old. ▶

READING THE ROCKS

THE KAIBAB LIMESTONE IS A 300-FOOT (91.4 M) CLIFF-LIKE LAYER OF ROCKS FORMING THE RIM OF THE GRAND CANYON. IT'S KNOWN AS THE KAIBAB FORMATION, AND IT'S VISIBLE FROM THE NORTH AND SOUTH RIMS.

DATING ROCKS

Geologists can tell how old the rocks in the Grand Canyon are using a **technique** called **radiometric** dating. All rocks have **radioactive** elements within them. Over time, these elements break down into tiny particles called atoms. The elements break down at a fixed rate over time.

Each rock has its own radiometric clock. The clock starts when the rock forms. As time passes, the elements break down. To figure out a rock's age, a geologist needs to measure how much one of its elements has broken down.

Radiometric dating can't be used on all rocks. Sedimentary rocks sometimes don't produce **absolute** radiometric results. When this is the case, geologists rely on relative dating. Relative dating determines the age of a rock layer based on information about other nearby layers.

Geologists are scientists who study Earth and how it formed. ▶

READING THE LAYERS

Geologists study the relative age of rock layers by arranging them into a stratigraphic column. This column shows the rocks in a formation. Rock layers are ordered from oldest at the bottom to youngest at the top.

The stratigraphic column is based on the principle that a younger rock layer always forms on top of an older one. Therefore, rocks on the lowest layer formed earlier than those above them. According to this principle, the lowest layer is the oldest. In the Grand Canyon, it's the basement rock. The youngest layer is the uppermost layer— the Kaibab Limestone.

Combining the known radiometric dates and relative dates according to a stratigraphic column helps scientists piece together how old each of the rock layers are.

Layers of sedimentary rock are always horizontal, or from side to side. If they appear tilted, scientists know it's because a geological event occurred to make them shift.

FINDING FOSSILS

Fossils are another clue scientists use to determine the age of rocks. The sedimentary layers of the Grand Canyon contain rich fossil records from 740 million to 1,200 million years ago. Some common fossils include ferns, corals, scorpions, and animal tracks. The fossils tell us about where the rocks came from and what was going on at the point in history at which they formed.

The Grand Canyon fossils can be divided into two groups—marine, or sea, fossils, and terrestrial, or land, fossils. The oldest marine fossils are stromatolites, formed by layers of slimy sea bacteria. Later, shelled organisms called brachiopods appeared. The terrestrial fossils of leaves, animal tracks, and dragonflies formed during the Paleozoic era 525 million to 270 million years ago.

READING THE ROCKS

THERE ARE NO DINOSAUR FOSSILS AT THE GRAND CANYON. THAT'S BECAUSE THE ROCKS MAKING UP THE GRAND CANYON WERE FORMED BEFORE DINOSAURS WALKED THE EARTH. HOWEVER, THE CANYON ITSELF FORMED AFTER DINOSAURS WENT EXTINCT.

It is illegal to take fossils from Grand Canyon National Park. Fossils are important historical records for scientists to study and for all to see.

A GEOLOGICAL TIME CAPSULE

The Grand Canyon is more than a beautiful landmark—it's a record of geological history, which includes more than a billion years of fossil history! By examining the rock layers of the Grand Canyon, scientists can better understand ancient plants and animals, how the landscape changed over time, and how geological forces have shaped the earth and may do so in the future.

SHIFTING UPWARD

The Kaibab Limestone is the topmost rock layer in the Grand Canyon. Based on radiometric dating, relative dating, and fossil identification, geologists have determined that this limestone likely was once an ocean floor. How exactly did the rock layer move from the ocean bottom to 9,000 feet (2,743.2 m) above sea level? The planet pushed it upward.

This geologic activity occurs in the **lithosphere**. This layer is made up of tectonic plates that float and move on top of a layer of soft rock. When the plates bump into each other, rocks on Earth's surface shift.

Between 30 million and 70 million years ago, this activity changed the landscape of the Grand Canyon's rock layers. The bumping plates pushed the rock layers upward, lifting the land and creating what's called the Colorado **Plateau**.

CONTINENTAL DRIFT

The continents that we know today were all once part of a supercontinent called Pangaea. Pangaea was a huge landmass that broke apart into pieces over time. The movement of tectonic plates caused the continents to shift. If you look closely at a map of Earth, you can imagine how the continents once fit together. Earth's plates continue to move today, crashing into and pulling away from each other. This movement is where many kinds of geologic activity begin.

CARVING THE CANYON

The rock layers of the Grand Canyon began to form almost 2 billion years ago, but the canyon is much younger. The Colorado River, which carved the canyon, began winding its way through the area about 5 million to 6 million years ago.

The huge canyon that we see today was caused by erosion. Erosion is a process in which the forces of wind, water, or ice wear away land. The water in the Colorado River cut into the rock layers, wearing them away and carving out the deep, wide canyon we see today. This process is called downcutting.

The river's large volume of water and fast current, or flow, made it a very powerful force. It pulled large rocks down and carried them away.

CURRENT AND VOLUME

The Colorado River is about 300 feet (91.4 m) across and 40 feet (12.2 m) deep. On average, its water flows at a rate of 12,000 to 15,000 cubic feet (339.8 to 424.8 cubic m) per second. Over its 277-mile (445.8 km) course, it flows down a slope of about 2,000 feet (609.6 m). Millions of years ago, when it carved out the canyon, its powerful waters flowed faster than they do now.

The ancient Colorado River continues to change the landscape of the Grand Canyon today.

DATING THE RIVER

The Colorado River is younger than the rocks that form the canyon's walls, and the canyon itself is younger than the Colorado River. How have geologists come to the conclusion that the Colorado River began to carve out the canyon 5 million to 6 million years ago?

As the river carved out the canyon, it also deposited, or left behind, sediment. Geologists have used these rock deposits to date the Colorado River. The idea is that rocks deposited by the river are younger than the river. Rocks not deposited by the river are older than the river. Therefore, the age of the river is somewhere between the age of the rocks that were deposited and those that weren't, which is between 5 million and 6 million years old.

Since the Colorado River created the Grand Canyon, the canyon is younger than the river.

AN ONGOING PROCESS

From the formation of the basement rock 1.8 billion years ago to the carving of the canyon 5 million to 6 million years ago, natural processes have greatly transformed the landscape of the Grand Canyon. Although you may not be able to tell just by looking at it, the Grand Canyon is still changing today.

The forces that created the Grand Canyon are still at work. Weathering and erosion from rain and snowfall affect the Grand Canyon every year. The Colorado River continues to deepen the canyon through downcutting. At times in the past, volcanic eruptions have changed the flow of the river, blocking the water and creating lakes. During the 1900s, 45 different earthquakes shook the Grand Canyon. These processes will shape the canyon's future.

READING THE ROCKS

THE CAVE OF THE DOMES IS IN THE GRAND CANYON. IN ADDITION TO NATURE'S CLUES TO ITS LOCATION, HIKERS HAVE ALSO LEFT BEHIND CLUES. IN THE PAST, SOME HIKERS SIGNED THE CAVE WALLS.

What could the Grand Canyon
look like in a few million years?

THE HISTORY OF THE GRAND CANYON

Historically, Native American groups inhabited the area around the Grand Canyon. Evidence of the first people there dates back 12,000 years. Early hunter-gatherers lived there until 1,000 BC and, by 500 BC, a group of farming people lived in the area. Today, there are 11 Native American groups traditionally associated with the Grand Canyon.

The first Europeans to arrive in the area were Spanish explorers. During the late 1800s, residents of the United States began to explore the region. In 1893, President Benjamin Harrison labeled the area a forest reserve. In 1908, President Theodore Roosevelt made the Grand Canyon a national monument. In 1919, Congress officially made it a national park.

READING THE ROCKS

JOHN WESLEY POWELL, AN AMERICAN GEOLOGIST, EXPLORED THE GRAND CANYON IN 1869 AND 1871. HE STUDIED AND NAMED MANY OF THE GRAND CANYON'S FEATURES AND CREATED THE FIRST RELIABLE MAPS OF THE COLORADO RIVER.

Archeological artifacts from a number of Native American cultures, including those of the Zuni, Hopi, Navajo, and Southern Paiute peoples, have been found near the Grand Canyon.

ECOLOGICAL IMPORTANCE

Hundreds of animal species live in Grand Canyon National Park, including about 400 bird species, about 90 mammal species, about 20 fish species, and about 60 reptile and amphibian species. Bats, bighorn sheep, coyotes, elk, mountain lions, rattlesnakes, and scorpions are just a few of the animals there. Seven endangered species, including the California condor, live in the canyon. There are more than 1,750 plant species and more than 8,000 known species of insects.

The many kinds of wildlife within Grand Canyon National Park make it very important ecologically. There are five different ecosystems within the park. From the evergreen-covered boreal forest ecosystem on the North Rim to the dry, hot desert scrub ecosystem at the bottom of the canyon, the huge park covers a number of very different environments.

This bighorn sheep is one kind of mammal that makes its home in the Grand Canyon. ▶

ELK

BIGHORN SHEEP

CONSERVING THE CANYON

The Grand Canyon is often considered one of the seven natural wonders of the world. In 2019, Grand Canyon National Park reached 100 years as a national park. But despite its age and rock-solid foundation, this special place is at risk.

Human activity—not the forces of time—threatens the Grand Canyon most. The main threats to the canyon include noise, air, water, and soil pollution. Nearby coal plants and mining operations pollute the surrounding ecosystems. Building developments to improve park tourism also pose a threat to sacred Native American lands and waterways.

We must work to make sure that this ancient landmark stands the test of time. You can help protect the future of the Grand Canyon by sharing what you've learned.

Park rangers are committed to guarding the Grand Canyon and teaching the public about its history.

A TRULY GRAND PLACE

The Grand Canyon didn't appear overnight. Its rocks began to take shape nearly 2 billion years ago with the formation of the Vishnu schist. Over the course of millions of years, layers of sediment became layers of rock. The heavy stone layers were pushed upward by the force of tectonic movement. Finally, the Colorado River carved its way through the rock, molding the great canyon we know today. Many visitors each year delight in the canyon's natural beauty.

This geological wonder is rich in cultural history and geological significance. One only needs to look at it to sense its greatness. As John Wesley Powell once said: "The wonders of the Grand Canyon cannot be **adequately** represented in symbols of speech, nor by speech itself."

GLOSSARY

absolute: Not to be doubted or questioned.

adequate: To an acceptable degree.

artifact: Something made by humans in the past that still exists.

cultural: Having to do with the beliefs and ways of life of a group of people.

gorge: A narrow valley between hills or mountains, typically with rocky walls and water running through it.

heritage: The traditions and beliefs that are part of the history of a group or nation.

iconic: Having to do with being symbolic or a representative of a certain idea.

lithosphere: The layer of Earth that includes the crust and upper mantle.

plateau: A broad, flat, raised area of land.

radioactive: Giving off rays of light, heat, or energy.

radiometric: Relating to the measurement of radioactivity.

reliable: Able to be trusted.

technique: A particular skill or ability that someone uses to perform a job.

unique: One of a kind.

INDEX

WEBSITES

Due to the changing nature of Internet links, PowerKids Press has developed an online list of websites related to the subject of this book. This site is updated regularly. Please use this link to access the list: www.powerkidslinks.com/EHTR/canyon